O9-BUD-150

The Lighthouses of Maine

Text and photography by Wally Welch

The most complete pictorial guide
presently available of the historic lighthouses
of the coast of Maine.

Foreword

The lighthouse has had a significant role in the marine history of our country. Losses of many ships and men occurred prior to the development of our lighthouse system. Once the value of the lights was seen, priority was given to their establishment. I like this story which illustrates the preeminence of the lighthouse.

> *A ship in the darkness of a foggy night thought another ship was approaching and signaled for it to change course 10 degrees to the south. The reply came asking instead that the ship sending the message change course 10 degrees to the north. Irritated, the captain of the ship repeated, "Change course 10 degrees to the south". For effect he added, "I am a captain!" This time the answer came back, "Change your course 10 degrees to the north, I am a boatswain." "Change your course 10 degrees to the south", the captain ordered and added "I am a battleship!" The exchange ended when the boatswain confidently stated, "Change your course 10 degrees to the north, I am a lighthouse"!*

Several good books give historical and technical information on the lighthouses of the Maine Coast. Some give photographic and geographic information. In our search for an accurate photographic record of all the lighthouses in Maine, we discovered that none listed all of the lighthouses, and none included photographs of them all.

In seeking information about Maine's lighthouses, we found there was quite a lot of interest in a complete and accurate book. This book is our first attempt to fill that need. Our objective is to provide more of a pictorial guide than a historical one. We do include, however, brief historical information that we feel will be of interest to the reader.

We are including lights which are or have been residences without regard to whether the light is currently active.

Lights which are merely beacons on skeleton towers are not included, even though they are found among lights currently listed by the Coast Guard.

A few lights which are not strictly Maine lights are listed, inasmuch as they are seen from Maine.

Lights are listed generally in the geographic order in which they occur from south to north.

Each of these sites has been personally visited to take these pictures. Visiting the locations, getting a feel of the setting, and talking to the people in the area has been one of our most rewarding and enjoyable experiences.

Our only regret is that we didn't get started on this project sooner so that we could have met more of the lighthouse keepers themselves. In a very few years all of the lights will be automated and lighthouse families will become extinct. At present they are an endangered species. As we recall, only about ten of the lights in Maine are presently manned by U.S. Coast Guard personnel. Several of these have told us that the lights where they are stationed are scheduled to be automated and will no longer be manned by the Coast Guard.

We would encourage you to visit as many of the lights as possible. You can drive to many of them. Some require you to get a lobster fisherman to take you in his boat. Others, you may have to fly over in a rented airplane. We found "Mainers" very helpful and supportive in this respect.

The lighthouse enthusiast will want to visit museums in Maine that feature lighthouses, their artifacts, and history. They are: The Shore Village Museum in Rockland, The Marine Museum at Bath, The Marine Museum at Searsport, and the Museums located in lighthouses at Pemaquid Point and Monhegan Island. Helpful lighthouse information and good association may also be obtained through the U.S. Lighthouse Society, 130 St. Elmo Way, San Francisco, CA 94127 (415) 584-9748.

Most of you will probably visit the lights only through the pages of this book, but good luck to those who take on such a project. However you see them, we hope you will have as much fun learning about the lights as we have!

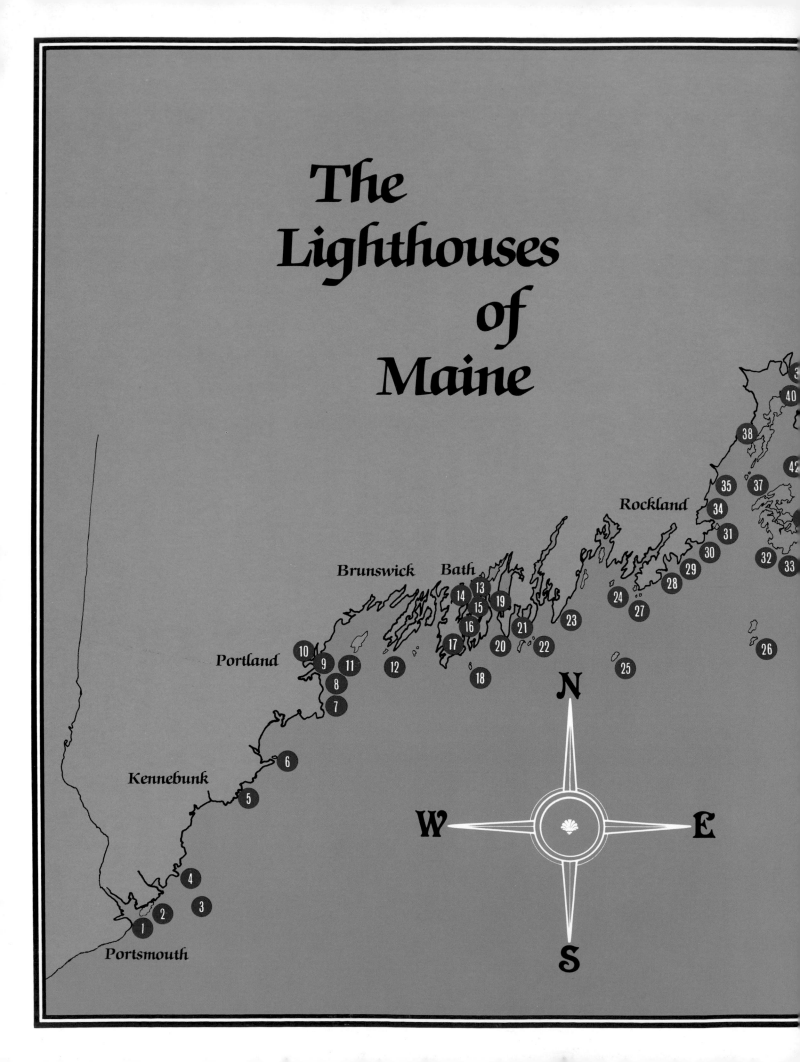

Lubec

Machias

Bar
Harbor

INDEX

1. WHALEBACK LIGHT
(white light flashing twice each ten seconds)

This lighthouse, built in 1820, has born the brunt of many severe storms. The original tower, badly damaged by heavy seas, was replaced by a new tower completed in 1872. Although this light is often listed as being in New Hampshire (since it protects the Portsmouth harbor), it is actually closer to the Maine coast. It is best seen from Fort Foster which is reached from Kittery, Maine.

2. FORT CONSTITUTION LIGHT
(New Hampshire)

This light can be seen quite well from Fort Foster, Maine. It marks the inner harbor of Portsmouth and is seen from the same point as is Whaleback Light.

3. BOON ISLAND LIGHT
(white occulting light flashing every 30 seconds)

Located 6½ miles southeast of Cape Neddick, this light is considered to be one of the most isolated lights along the Maine coast. The original wooden tower built on this rocky ledge in 1811 was washed away in a severe storm typical of the area. It was replaced by a stone tower which was also swept away in a storm in 1855. The 133-foot granite tower which replaced the second tower still stands. It is the tallest of the lights along the Maine coast. In clear weather it can easily be seen from Nubble Light at Cape Neddick.

Before the turn of the century Boon Island Light became a stag station inasmuch as it was considered too dangerous for women and children. William Williams served as keeper of this lonely station for 27 years.

4. CAPE NEDDICK LIGHT
(red light flashing every six seconds)

This light commonly known as Nubble is one of the more popular lights of the Maine coast. Its proximity to shore at Cape Neddick has made it one of the most visited lights. It is at the north end of York Beach and can be reached 1.1 miles off Route 1A at the end of Nubble Road. In fair weather it would be possible, though not allowed in recent years, to wade to the island at low tide. The original tower built in 1879 still stands. In recent years keeper Bob French has beautified the station by adding holiday lights around the house and out-buildings.

Historical highlights include accounts of a keeper who was relieved of his duties for a sideline of ferrying visitors to the island for a fee. A baby was born at this station. The daughter of one of the keepers of this light was married in the lantern room at the top of the light tower.

5. GOAT ISLAND LIGHT
(white light flashing every six seconds)

This lighthouse, built in 1822 and rebuilt in 1859, is located at the southwest end of Goat Island near the entrance of Cape Porpoise Harbor. The popular resort of Kennebunkport is nearby. It is reached from US 1 on Highway 9. It can be seen and photographed quite easily from the fishing docks at the end of the road.

6. WOOD ISLAND LIGHT
(white light flashing twice at six-second intervals)

This light was built in 1808 on the east end of Wood Island. It is just off from the village of Biddeford Pool and also marks the mouth of the Saco River.

The island is no longer wooded due to being deforested by high winds and fire. Once the scene of a murder, the island is claimed by some to be haunted by the ghost of the murdered victim.

In the mid 1800's lighthouse keeper Thomas Orcutt had a famous dog named Sailer. He was known for his faithfulness at ringing the fog bell to warn passing ships of the island's rocky shore.

There is presently no lantern room on the light, the conical tower having only a beacon type globe at its top. In this respect it is similar to the Mount Desert Rock Light.

7. CAPE ELIZABETH LIGHT
(white light with six flashes at 30-second intervals)

Originally built in 1829 as one of Maine's two locations having two light towers, this station was first called "Two Lights". The top of the westernmost light was dismantled in 1924 when the government ruled that all lights should be converted to single beacons. In 1985 this inactive light was refurbished and given a new top by its private owners. Matinicus Rock was the sight of Maine's other twin light.

The Cape Elizabeth Light is easily accessible just off Highway 77 near Two Lights State Park. The light is automated and the dwelling is now a private residence. One of the most beautiful, this light is also the most powerful on the New England Coast. Its light is visible for 27 miles.

8. PORTLAND HEAD LIGHT   (next page)
(white light flashing each 3.7 seconds)

This is Maine's oldest light. It was built by direction of George Washington in 1791. Because of its beauty, historical significance, and proximity to Portland, this light station is one of the most highly visited lights in New England.

This sentinel to Maine's busiest harbor has been witness to many a shipwreck. Some twenty vessels were destroyed in a great storm in 1869 when the fog bell was destroyed by giant waves. The well remembered storm of April 3, 1975, not only battered the wall of the whistle house, but knocked out the foghorn and temporarily extinguished the beacon as well.

Famous names are often associated with this light. Henry Wadsworth Longfellow wrote many lines of poetry while visiting this favorite spot. John E. Fitzgerald, maternal grandfather of John, Robert and Edward Kennedy, had less pleasant memories of this site. He was one of the survivors of the ship "Bohcmian" whlch split her hull open on nearby rocks. Nearly 40 of the ship's 318 passengers and crew were drowned when their lifeboat dumped them into the turbulent winter seas while being launched. An immigrant lad at the time in 1864, Fitzgerald later became the mayor of Boston.

Portland Head Light is adjacent to Fort Williams State Park and may be reached from U.S. 1 on 1A, 77, and the Shore Road to Cape Elizabeth.

Perhaps Longfellow was describing the view of Rams Island Ledge Light from this favorite spot at Portland Head Light when he wrote the following poem.

The Lighthouse

The rocky ledge runs far into the sea,
and on its outer point, some miles away,
The lighthouse lifts its massive masonry,
A pillar of fire by night, of cloud by day.

Even at this distance I can see the tides,
Upheaving, break unheard along its base,
A speechless wrath, that rises and subsides
In the white lip and tremor of the face.

And as the evening darkens, lo! how bright,
through the deep purple of the twilight air,
Beams forth the sudden radiance of its light
With strange, unearthly splendor in the glare!

Not one alone; from each projecting cape
And perilous reef along the ocean's verge,
Starts into life a dim, gigantic shape,
Holding its lantern o'er the restless surge.

Like the great giant Christopher it stands
Upon the brink of the tempestous wave,
Wading far out among the rocks and sands,
The night-O'ertaken mariner to save.

And the great ships sail outward and return
Bending and bowing o'er the billowy swells,
And ever joyful, as they see it burn,
They wave their silent welcomes and farewells.

They come forth from the darkness, and their sails
Gleam for a moment only in the blaze,
And eager faces, as the light unveils,
Gaze at the tower, and vanish while they gaze.

The mariner remembers when a child,
On his first voyage, he saw it fade and sink;
And when returning from adventures wild,
He saw it rise again o'er ocean's brink.

Steadfast, serene, immovable, the same
Year after year, through all the silent night
Burns on forevermore that quenchless flame,
Shines on that inextinguishable light!

It seems the ocean to its bosom clasp
The rocks and sea-sand with the kiss of peace;
It sees the wild winds lift it in their grasp,
And hold it up, and shake it like a fleece.

The startled waves leap over it; the storm
Smites it with all the scourges of the rain,
And steadily against its solid form
Press the great shoulders of the hurricane.

The sea-bird wheeling round it, with the din
Of wings and winds and solitary cries,
Blinded and maddened by the light within,
Dashes himself against the glare, and dies.

A new Prometheus, chained upon the rock,
Still grasping in his hand the fire of Jove,
It does not hear the cry, nor heed the shock,
But hails the mariner with words of love.

"Sail on!" it says, "sail on, ye stately ships!
And with your floating bridge the ocean span;
Be mine to guard this light from all eclipse.
Be yours to bring man nearer unto man!"

by Henry Wadsworth Longfellow

9. SPRING POINT LEDGE LIGHT (light flashes every 6 seconds and has 2 red sectors)

This light is located in South Portland in old Fort Preble vicinity.
It is on a breakwater-type protrusion on the west side of the main channel to Portland Harbor. Built in 1897, it was originally surrounded by water until the 900-foot breakwater was built to it from shore in 1951. The unusual design of this light is similar to the Goose Rocks and Lubec Channel lights.

10. PORTLAND BREAKWATER LIGHT

First built in 1855, the original wooden light tower was built by order of the United States Lighthouse Board. It was replaced by the present cast iron tower in 1875. A keeper's dwelling was added against the light tower in 1889.

During World War II land was filled in for shipbuilding activity which extended the shore to the light station. It had been nearly a third of a mile out in the harbor on a breakwater.

The first light which was a fixed red signal later was changed to a flashing red light.

11. RAM ISLAND LEDGE LIGHT (white light flashes twice each ten seconds)

This light built in 1905 is located at the north side of the entrance to Portland Harbor. It is built on a jagged stretch of rock which is visible only at low tide. This light can be seen easily from Portland Head Light.

The tower is a gray granite and has the appearance of being very old even though it is one of the more recently built lights.

19

12. HALFWAY ROCK LIGHT
(red light flashes every 5 seconds)

Halfway Rock is located in a much-used shipping lane. It was a treacherous three-acre outcropping of rock prior to the light's completion in 1871. The light and the huge bell, replaced by a foghorn in 1905, have doubtless prevented many disastrous shipwrecks since being established.

Its name comes from being half way between Cape Elizabeth and Small Point at the opposite ends of Casco Bay. This light approximately ten miles north east of Portland was severely damaged in a violent storm of February 1972. The wooden walkway, the generator and fuel tank and part of the boathouse were washed away. With no power for the light or for heat, the crew was removed by helicopter.

13. DOUBLING POINT LIGHT
(white light flashes every 4 seconds)

This light, built in 1898, is one of four on the Kennebec River guiding ships from the Atlantic to the shipbuilding town of Bath. The light is a white wooden octagonal tower built on a square concrete pier. It is the light closest to Bath and is near the upper end of Fiddler Reach.

The light and wooden walkway to shore can be seen across the river on Highway 209, a short distance south of Bath. It may also be reached by taking Highway 127 south 1.8 miles from U.S. 1 to a dirt road on the right marked "Doubling Point Road".

14. KENNEBEC RIVER LIGHT
(Two beacon towers—front beacon with quick white flash, rear beacon with equal 6-second intervals of light and dark)

This light, built in 1908, has two small wooden towers with beacons lined up in such a way as to indicate the middle of the river channel to a ship's captain. It was formerly called Doubling Point Range Light.

In 1982 this light became the only one in the country tended by a woman resident keeper. Karen McLain, who lives at this light with her boat captain husband, also is the keeper of the nearby Doubling Point and Squirrel Point Lights. These two lights also on the Kennebec are automated, as is the Kennebec River Light.

The Kennebec River Light can be reached by following same road as to the Doubling Point Light and taking the left fork marked Kennebec River Light.

15. SQUIRREL POINT LIGHT
(fixed red light with white sector)

This light is a small white wooden tower with a single room and wooden walkway attached. The keeper's dwelling is nearby. The keepers formerly had to boat their children across the river to Phippsburg to school. Now Squirrel Point Light is automated and the keeper lives at the Kennebec River Light.

Squirrel Point may be seen directly across the river from Phippsburg which is on Highway 209. It may be reached by taking Highway 127 to Steen Road just north of the Arrowsic-Georgetown Bridge. There will be about one-half mile of paved road to Bald Head Road. From Bald Head Road there is about an .8 mile footpath to the lighthouse.

16. PERKINS ISLAND
(red light with 2 white sectors flashing each 2.5 seconds)

This light is also on the eastern side of the Kennebec River. It is most easily seen from the village of Parker Head. The village is reached by traveling south out of Phippsburg on an unmarked paved road which follows the river. The white wooden octoganal tower built in 1898 is accompanied by a keeper's house, barn, and large stone belltower.

17. POND ISLAND
(white light with 6-second intervals of light and dark)

This light is now only a white conical tower on the island just to the west of the Kennebec River mouth. It can be seen from Highway 209 near Fort Popham and Popham Beach. It is automated and the former dwelling and out-buildings have been destroyed.

18. SEGUIN
(fixed white light)

Built in 1795, the original wooden tower was replaced by stone in 1819 and rebuilt again in 1857. Although the tower is a relatively stubby 53 feet, it is the highest above the water on the Maine coast.

Its original first order lens is one of the most powerful on the coast. It has been estimated that to replace this prism type lens which focuses the light would cost several millions of dollars.

Because of often-heavy fog, this light station has one of the most powerful foghorns made. One keeper claimed that the horn was so powerful that he had seen seagulls knocked from the sky by its blast.

Located two miles south of the mouth of the Kennebec River, this light can be seen from shore in the Popham Beach area reached from Bath on Route 209. Tour boats from Boothbay Harbor also pass by it, as well as other lights in the area.

19. HENDRICKS HEAD LIGHT
(fixed white light with a red sector)

Built in 1829 and rebuilt in 1875, this light is located west of Southport on the east side of the mouth of the Sheepscot River. This was the site of one of the most amazing lighthouse rescue accounts. From this location comes the story of the rescue and adoption by the lighthouse keeper family of a tiny infant who washed ashore in a violent storm. The baby, the only survivor of the wreck, was found in a box bound between feather tick mattresses for protection.

20. THE CUCKOLDS LIGHT
(white light flashing twice each 6 seconds)

This station was originally established as a fog signal location in 1892. In 1907 a light tower was added on top of the fog signal house. It is less than a mile off the tip of Southport Island and the village of Newagen. It is on a very small wave-swept island which has no soil whatever. Before the fog signal and light were established, the rock was a serious threat to the heavy traffic entering Boothbay Harbor.

continued

20. THE CUCHOLDS LIGHT *(cont'd.)*

This light can be seen from Newagen and from the tour boats from Boothbay Harbor. Newagen is reached by following Route 27 from U.S. 1.

21. BURNT ISLAND LIGHT
(red light flashing each 6 seconds—2 white sectors)

This light on the west side of the entrance to Boothbay Harbor can be seen by sailors only after passing the Cucholds light. It was built in 1821 and altered in 1888 so that its light would not attract ships over the rocks at Cucholds which were in the path to the Burnt Island Light. It can be seen from the mainland on the east side of the harbor or from the tour boats from the harbor. Routes 27 and 96 should be followed from U.S. 1 for this purpose.

22. RAM ISLAND
(fixed red light with 2 white sectors)

This light, built in 1883, is on the Ram Island off Ocean Point on the eastern side of the mouth of Boothbay Harbor. The station is located on Linekin Neck on the south side of Fisherman Island Passage. The long walkway originally bridging the tower to the Island has been destroyed in recent years.

23. PEMAQUID POINT LIGHT
(white light flashing every six seconds)

This light, built in 1827, is located on the western side of Muscongus Bay. From Route U.S. 1 it can be reached from Newcastle and Damariscotta on Route 130, which ends at Pemaquid Point. The town has developed a parking and picnic area at the lighthouse. There is also a fine museum which features lighthouse and nautical items.

The lighthouse sits astride a unique rock formation which shows the devastation of the waves which pound this area in strong winds. Due to having tillable land in the area of the lighthouse, the keepers were expected to help provide for themselves by farming. The first keeper, Isaac Dunham, built several barns and out-buildings during his ten years at the station. These buildings were to be a subject of controversy for future keepers since they were asked to reimburse their predecessor for their current value.

A violent storm September 16 of 1903 claimed lives of several seamen in this area. Captain Willard Poole and thirteen of his crew of the fishing schooner George F. Edmunds were lost, with only two of his crew surviving. The ships Sadie and Lillie were also destroyed in the storm, with only two men surviving.

24. FRANKLIN ISLAND
(white light flashing every six seconds)

The present light, built in 1855, is on the northwest side of Franklin Island in Muscongus Bay. It replaced a marker placed there as a navigational aid in 1805. The light is most easily reached by boat from the village of Friendship. Heavy rain and high seas marked our visit and prevented us from getting very close to this small island facing the open ocean. The keeper's dwelling and buildings, other than the light tower, have all been removed.

25. MONHEGAN ISLAND LIGHT
(white light flashing for 2.8 seconds every 30 seconds)

This light was built in 1824 on Monhegan Island, which was Maine's earliest fishing village. It was first established as a fishing village and refuge from the Indians in 1614. The light, located near the center of the island on high ground, is second highest above water in the state. Seguin is only two feet higher at 180 feet. A museum is in the former house where the lightkeepers lived. Tourist accommodations are available on the island, and both air and boat transportation are available from Port Clyde. The island is approximately ten miles south of Port Clyde.

26. MATINICUS ROCK LIGHT
(white light flashing once, and then twice, each 15 seconds)

Built in 1827, this light is situated on a 30-acre barren rock, six miles south of Matinicus Island. Twenty five miles from Rockland — the nearest port — this light station is probably the most isolated of all those along the coast of Maine. The two original wooden light towers were replaced by stone towers in 1848. In 1924 it became a single light tower by government order, as did other double light stations. The old tower still remains with its lantern room top having been dismantled.

Being far out to sea, Matinicus Rock experiences some of the most violent storms of any inhabited location. It has also been a light where keepers have been credited with some of the most heroic acts.

Best known heroine of Matinicus Rock Light was keeper's daughter Abbie Burgess. She was credited with saving her invalid mother and three sisters during a violent storm which swept over the rock in January of 1856. Her older brother was no longer at home and the father had gone to the mainland for provisions. Abbie had taken the family into the base of the lighthouse tower for safety when the storm swept away the residence in which they had been living.

During this storm, which kept her father away for four weeks, 17-year-old Abbie cared for her mother and sisters and never let the lights fail during the entire time.

Several years later, when her father was replaced as keeper, Abbie stayed to help them learn the chores to be cared for on Matinicus. At 22, she fell in love with the keeper's son and was married to him within the year. She was appointed with him to be an assistant keeper of the twin lights.

In 1875 the two of them with their four children born on Matinicus were transferred to the Whitehead Light station some twenty miles away. Here they served as keepers for 15 years. Abbie became known throughout her life for her conscientiousness in keeping the lights. It seemed to be the great concern of her life. When she died, she was honored by a large group, including a governor of one of the New England states. At her request, her burial spot was marked with a tombstone made in the shape of a lighthouse.

27. MARSHALL POINT LIGHT
(a fixed white light)

This light, built in 1832 and rebuilt in 1857, is located in Port Clyde. It can be reached from Thomaston by following Routes U.S. 1 and 131 to Port Clyde. The light marks the eastern side of the south entrance to Port Clyde Harbor.

28. TENANTS HARBOR LIGHT
(not a functioning light)

This lighthouse now privately owned can be seen from shore in the village of Tenants Harbor. Turn left at East Wind Inn and follow this road along the shore for a good view of Southern Island and the light station.

29. WHITEHEAD LIGHT
(a green light occulting every four seconds)

This light, built originally in 1807 and rebuilt in 1852, is on a small island near Tenants Harbor. It can be seen only from the air or from a boat. It was the station to which Abbie Burgess Grant and her husband Isaac moved to from Matinicus Rock in 1875.

This being one of the foggiest areas on the coast, a foghorn has always been a part of the history of this light station. For a time a foghorn driven by a mechanism, wound up by the movement of the tide, operated here.

An embarrassing scandal was experienced at The Whitehead Light during its first years of operation. The first keeper was found to be guilty of selling what he purported to be surplus whale oil to many of the prominent local citizens of Thomaston. The lighthouse keeper was dishonorably discharged after an inspection was made by the government to see why so much oil was being used.

30. TWO BUSH ISLAND LIGHT
(white light with a red sector flashing every five seconds)

This light, built in 1897, is just outside the west side of Penobscot Bay. It is almost directly south of Owls Head Light Station.

31. OWLS HEAD LIGHT
(fixed white light)

This light, built in 1826, is on a promonotory south of Rockland Harbor. The light and foghorn of this station have been very important to this heavily sailed entry to Rockland. This area has been the site of many wrecks during severe storms.

In the 1930's, keeper Augustus Hamer's dog Spot was credited with guiding the Matinicus mailboat safely past the peninsula by his incessant barking. The fogbell which the dog would ring by tugging at its rope, was fouled by snowdrifts from the storm which was raging. Hearing the boat's whistle, he seemed to sense it might crash into the rocks of Owls Head without the sound to guide its captain. Spot is reported to be buried near the present light and foghorn.

The light is easily reached from Rockland by following Route 73 south just under two miles to a left turn which follows the shore line to Owls Head. A left turn just past the post office will lead to the lighthouse.

32. HERON NECK LIGHT
(fixed red light with a white sector)

This light, built in 1854, is on Green's Island, a small island just southwest of Carver's Harbor at Vinalhaven Island. It is on the east side of Hurricane Sound and is most easily reached from Vinalhaven. It cannot be seen from Vinalhaven.

33. BROWNS HEAD LIGHT
(fixed white light with two red sectors)

This light, built in 1832 and rebuilt in 1857, is located on the northwest point of Vinalhaven Island. It is at the western end of Fox Island Thorofare. Auto and passenger ferries run to Vinalhaven from Rockland. The lighthouse can be reached by car by following the road to the northwest end of the island. Crockett River Road on the left will also have a Browns Head Light sign. The second right turn will take you to the lighthouse. This light is maintained by a U.S. Coast Guard family.

34. ROCKLAND BREAKWATER LIGHT
(white light flashing every five seconds)

Located on a stone jetty extending south from Jamison's point to protect Rockland Harbor, this light was built in 1888 and rebuilt in 1902. Heavy traffic into Rockland Harbor make this light and its foghorn very important. Waldo Road and Samoset Road can be followed to the light from Route U.S. 1 just north of Rockland.

35. INDIAN ISLAND LIGHT
(Called Graves light by some guides)

This former lighthouse is located at the eastern end of Rockport Harbor. It can be seen from the Rockport Marine Park. The property is now privately owned and is not operated as a light.

36. GOOSE ROCKS LIGHT
(red light flashing every 6 seconds, with white sector)

This "spark plug" light, built in 1890, is between Vinalhaven and North Haven Islands. It is at the eastern entrance of the Fox Islands Thorofare. Its shape is similar to the lights at Lubec Channel and Spring Point Ledge. It is automated and accessible only by boat or air.

37. CURTIS ISLAND LIGHT
(fixed green light)

This light, built in 1836 and rebuilt in 1896, is on the south side of the entrance to Camden Harbor. This light has been called Negro Island Light in the past. It may be seen by taking the road in front of the Camden Post Office south to Penobscot Avenue. A left on Penobscot and a right at the next stop sign to the barricade, then bearing left to the first two houses on the left, will put you in view of the lighthouse.

38. GRINDLE POINT LIGHT
(green light flashing every 4 seconds)

This light was built on Ilesboro Island in 1935. It can be reached by auto ferry from Lincolnville. The lighthouse is adjacent to the ferry landing. It is also distantly visible from the mainland. The light, now actually operating from a skeleton tower near the old abandoned light, is powered by solar-charged batteries.

39. FORT POINT LIGHT
(fixed white light)

This light was built in 1836 and rebuilt in 1857. It is built on a high point of land on the west side of the mouth of the Penobscot River. It is easily reached from Stockton Springs by following the signs to Fort Point State Park. A memorial and ruins of Fort Pownall may also be seen nearby.

One of the lighthouse stations still maintained by a U.S. Coast Guard family, this light still has the original prism lens built in France.

Boatswain Larry Baum was very helpful with information about this light.

40. DICE HEAD LIGHT
(white light flashing every six seconds)

The original lighthouse built in 1829 and rebuilt in 1937 is in the colorful village of Castine. The old lighthouse is now privately owned and the light operates from a skeleton tower at the water's edge. The light is reached by proceeding from Orland on U.S. 1 on Routes 175 and 166 to Castine. One mile past Fort George at the end of the road, the light will be visible. Castine is also the home of the Maine Maritime Academy.

41. PUMPKIN ISLAND LIGHT
(not now operational)

This light, built in 1854, has been privately owned since 1934. It is located at the northern end of Eggemoggin Reach, just off Little Deer Island. By turning right after crossing the Deer Island suspension bridge and continuing to the end of the road, the light can be seen on a small island just off shore.

42. EAGLE ISLAND LIGHT
(white light flashing every four seconds)

This light was built in 1839 and rebuilt in 1858. It is on the northeast end of the island, which is between Deer Isle and North Haven. It is in Penobscot Bay and is most easily reached by boat from the little village of Sunset between Deer Isle and Stonington. (We were grateful to ride with Robert Quinn in his boat "The Last Straw" to see this light).

43. DEER ISLAND THOROFARE/MARK ISLAND LIGHT
(white light flashing every six seconds)

This light, built in 1857, is on the west end of Mark Island. It can be seen distantly from the mainland at Stonington. West on Route 15, the light can be seen from Billings Marine Service and also points on the road beyond there.

44. ISLE AU HAUT LIGHT
(red light with white sector flashing each 4 seconds)

This light, built in 1907, is on Isle Au Haut south of Stonington. The island is a part of Acadia National Park and may be reached by ferry from Stonington. The dwelling portion of this station is now privately owned.

45. SADDLEBACK LEDGE LIGHT
(white light flashing each six seconds)

This light, built in 1839 on a small ledge of rock between Vinalhaven and Isle Au Haut, is one of the most remote of any on the Maine coast. When it was a manned station, it had the distinction of being the most difficult on which to make a landing. Landings on and off were accomplished by a boom and bosun's chair. Efforts to deposit soil here for gardening were discouraging, as the winter storms would take it away each year.

46. BURNT COAT HARBOR LIGHT/ HOCKAMOCK HEAD LIGHT

(green light occulting each 4 seconds)

This light, known by two different names, was built in 1872 at the entrance of Burnt Coat Harbor on the southwest tip of Swan's Island. Swan's Island can be reached by auto ferry from Bass Harbor on Mount Desert Island.

47. BLUE HILL BAY LIGHT
(green light flashing every 4 seconds)

This light, built in 1935, is on tiny Fly Island in Blue Hill Bay. It can be seen only by boat or airplane. The rocky island is quite flat and its dimensions change drastically with the tide.

48. BASS HARBOR HEAD LIGHT
(red light occulting every four seconds)

This light, built in 1858, is on the southwest point of Mount Desert Island. It marks the entrance of Blue Hill Bay and Bass Harbor. It is one of the most scenic and often visited lights in Maine. It is easily reached from Ellsworth by following Routes 3 and 102 to Bass Harbor.

49. GREAT DUCK ISLAND LIGHT
(red light flashing every 10 seconds)

Built in 1890 on the south end of the island, this light is not visible except by boat or airplane. It is about 5.5 miles southeast of Bass Harbor. Although the island is quite remote, it at one time boasted a one-teacher school. There were several keepers and one of them had sixteen children. During World War II a telephone cable was laid to the island so as to give prompt warning of enemy submarine sightings.

50. MT. DESERT ROCK LIGHT
(white light flashing every 15 seconds)

This light was built in 1830 on Mount Desert Rock. It is 20 miles south of Mount Desert Island and is one of the most remote lighthouses. It is another of the lights located on a rock island with no soil. Here, attempts were made to deposit soil for gardening. Again the results were disappointing. Waves often wash over the low-lying rocks. Lighthouse records indicate in one violent storm of 1842, a 54-ton stone was relocated by the waves.

51. BAKER ISLAND LIGHT
(white light flashing every ten seconds)

This light, built in 1828 and rebuilt in 1855, is on 123-acre Baker Island at the southwest entrance to Frenchman Bay. This beautifully wooded island is part of Acadia National Park.

52. BEAR ISLAND LIGHT
(light has been discontinued)

This light, built in 1839 and rebuilt in 1889, marked the entrance of Northeast Harbor on Mount Desert Island. The light has been replaced by lighted bouys. It is best seen by boat or from the air. Several charter boats available from Northeast Harbor pass this light.

53. EGG ROCK LIGHT
(red light flashing every five seconds)

This light, built in 1875, marks the entrance to Frenchman Bay. It is built on a relatively small rock island, so the light is on top of the house to conserve space. Avery Rock Light, built in the same year, had similar circumstances. The light tower and dwelling at Avery Rock, however, have now been dismantled.

In a Coast Guard renovation, the lantern room of Egg Rock Light was removed and airport type beacons were used to replace the prism type lenses. There were numerous complaints due to this change in appearance. Some have said it is the least attractive light on the coast. I can agree! This is unfortunate, too, because it is probably seen by all of the four million or so people visiting Acadia National Park each year. It stands in the middle of the entrance to Frenchman Bay in view of Cadillac Mountain and other scenic areas of Mount Desert Island.

54. WINTER HARBOR LIGHT

(not a functioning light)

This light, built in 1856, was sold to private owners in 1934. It is on Mark Island across Frenchman Bay from Bar Harbor. It can be seen from the highway on the western side of the Schoodic Peninsula. It is most easily reached by following Route 186 from U.S. 1 at West Gouldsboro south toward Schoodic Point. The Acadia National Park Picnic area is a good place to view it.

55. PROSPECT HARBOR POINT LIGHT

(red light with 2 white sectors flashing every 6 seconds)

This light, built in 1850 and rebuilt in 1891, is on the east side of the inner harbor. It is now part of a military base, but can be easily reached by following either Route 186 or 195 to Prospect Harbor. The road to Corea leads from the intersection of these two roads, and the lighthouse road is about two tenths of a mile down that road. There is also a good view from across the harbor. The keeper's house is now used as a guest house for the base.

56. PETIT MANAN LIGHT
(white light flashing every 10 seconds)

This light, built in 1817 and rebuilt in 1855, is on the east point of a small island 2½ miles off Petit Manan Point. It is next-to-the-tallest light in Maine, at 123 feet above the mean high water. (Tallest is Boon Island Light at 133 feet.) This station also has a fog signal to warn of the dangerous reef nearby. Repairs are often needed for the light tower due to the violent storms to which it is subjected. A second order lens previously in the tower can be seen at the Shore Village Museum in Rockland.

The wife of one keeper of this light requested to be the keeper after her husband's death. She was denied the request by the Lighthouse Department in Washington and another keeper was appointed.

57. NARRAGUAGUS LIGHT
(not a functioning light)

This light, called "Pond Island Light" by many of the local people, was built in 1856 on Pond Island in Narraguagus Bay. It has been privately owned since 1934. As with Petit Manan Light, it can only be reached by boat or air. I was grateful for the trip to the island from Millbridge in Lyndon Perry's 40-foot lobster boat "Foxy Lady".

58. NASH ISLAND LIGHT
(white light flashing every 6 seconds)

This light, built in 1838 and rebuilt in 1873, is on the east side of the mouth of Pleasant Bay near South Addison. This island once boasted a school for the keeper's large family. The light tower, all that remains of the station, is scheduled to be dismantled because the beacon has been replaced by a lighted buoy.

59. MOOSE PEAK LIGHT
(white light flashing every 30 seconds)

This light, built in 1827, is on the east side of Mistake Island and to the east of Great Wass Island south of Jonesport. As one of the foggiest areas along the coast, the station also contains a fog signal. This light of 1.1 million candlepower can be seen for 26 miles. It can be reached only by boat or air.

60. LIBBY ISLAND LIGHT
(white group light flashing every 20 seconds)

This light was built in 1817 on the southern tip of the island and marks the southern entrance of Machias Bay. Heavy fogs, often rolling in from the Bay of Fundy, make a foghorn necessary at this station, also. The most notable of many vessels which have wrecked in the area was the Nova Scotia schooner "Calendonia", whose captain ran it aground here in 1878.

61. MACHIAS SEAL ISLAND LIGHT
(white light flashing every 3 seconds)

This light station, only 12 miles off the Maine coast from Cutler, is maintained by the Canadian government. The Canadian Wildlife Service also has an officer there in the summers to study and protect the large colony of Puffins and other sea birds, such as Razorbill Auks, Storm Petrels and Terns.

62. LITTLE RIVER LIGHT
(white light flashing every 15 seconds)

This light, built in 1847 and rebuilt in 1975, is at the mouth of Little River and the entrance to Cutler Harbor. It can be seen only by boat or air, since it is on the sea side of a wooded offshore island.

63. WEST QUODDY HEAD LIGHT
(white group light flashing every 15 seconds)

This light, built in 1807 and rebuilt in 1858, is located on the easternmost point in the United States. It gets its "West" name from being west of East Quoddy Head Light (which is nearby in Canada). This light tower is remembered by its bright bands of red and white. Sandblasting of the tower in preparation for restoring its bright colors gave it an unexpected look for a time in 1985. The light is reached by following the Quoddy Head State Park signs from Route 189 just south of Lubec. Boatswain Mate 1st Class John Richardson, the officer in charge of this station, was helpful with information about the light.

64. EAST QUODDY HEAD LIGHT
(fixed red light)

This light is also known as Head Harbor Light. It is located on the northern end of Campobello Island in New Brunswick, Canada. The red cross design on the tower is typical of Canadian lights. This is said to make it more visible against a white background of snow.

This light can be reached by car and is approximately 18 miles from the border crossing. After a right turn a mile beyond Roosevelt Park, the road to the light is fairly well marked.

65. LUBEC CHANNEL LIGHT
(green light flashing every six seconds)

This light, built in 1890, is on the west side of the Lubec Channel. It can be seen on Route 189 going to the Canadian Border and also on the way to Quoddy Head State Park and West Quoddy Head Light. It was originally a manned stag station. It is now automated and it has been unmanned since one of the keepers died of fumes from a faulty heater.

66. MULHOLLAND LIGHT
(not a functioning light)

This light is on the east side of the Lubec Channel on Campobello Island. It is on the Canadian side on the left just past the Canadian customs station. We have included it since it is easily seen from the Maine side of the channel.

67. WHITLOCKS MILL LIGHT (green light with equal 6 second intervals of light & dark)

This light, built in 1892 and rebuilt in 1910, is on the south bank of the St. Croix River at Calais, Maine. It is found by counting five driveways back to the south from Taylor Furniture Store on U.S. 1, just south of Calais. The dwelling has recently been sold and is private property. It can also be seen in the distance from the roadside park just south on U.S. 1.

The light is the northernmost light and ends our pictorial tour of the lighthouses of the beautiful coast and rivers of Maine.

Epilogue

The symbolism of the lighthouse:

Savings companies have used it as a logo to portray safety and security.

Educational institutions have used this symbol to depict guidance and direction.

Churches sometimes use it to represent the light which leads to salvation.

Longfellow saw the lighthouse in poetic symbols and figures, as does my good neighbor and friend, Frank McMillan, whose verse about the lighthouse is also included.

The Lighthouse

The lighthouse
erected with no barrier
between it and
the mariner whom it will guide.
Its beam
constant, strong and true
often obscured by
storm,
mist and fog.
Still the haven
for the one who,
searching,
endures the elements
until light breaks through.

The lighthouse of God's love
originally given with no barrier
between Him and
the recipients of His goodness.
That light
forever steady,
often distorted by
untruths,
and misrepresentations.
Still gives peace and joy
to those who,
searching,
see it break through in
the life of the
Light of the World.

frank mcmillan

To me lighthouses symbolize the strength, faithfulness, and often the heroism, of their keepers. The conscientious giving of self for the benefit and safety of others is a portrayal I appreciate in the lighthouse.

The lights and their keepers are very special to us. We hope the lights and the symbolism associated with them are as meaningful to you. It would make us happy to further share with our readers in any way which we can. The "Light of the World" has done so much for us we are happy to share the spiritual blessings of His light, safety, and security with you.

Wally and Jo Welch
Linneal Beach Dr.
Apopka, Fla. 32703

Photographed and written by Wally Welch
Edited and produced by HealthAd, Orlando, FL.
Designed by Derek Dugan, Orlando, FL.
Printed by Southeastern Printing, Stuart, FL.
Separations by Dimension Inc., Tampa, FL.
Verse by Frank McMillan used by permission.

Poem, The Lighthouse, by Henry Wadsworth Longfellow is from
The Poetical Works of Longfellow, Cambridge Edition, 1975.
Houghton Mifflin Co. Boston. Used by permission.
Library of Congress Catalog #85-90214

ISBN 0-9618410-1-X